THE DARK SIDE

Ghosts
and Other Specters

illustrated by David West

and

written by Anita Ganeri

PowerKiDS press.

New York

Published in 2011 by The Rosen Publishing Group, Inc.
29 East 21st Street, New York, NY 10010

Designed and produced by
David West Books

Designer: Gary Jeffrey
Editor: Ronne Randall
U.S. Editor: Kara Murray
Illustrator: David West

Picture credits: 8b, Angelhead; 12b, 14l, Library of Congress; 15b, Pilgab; 20b, LuckyLouie; 21-22, Paul Keleher; 21b, Tomascastelazo

Library of Congress Cataloging-in-Publication Data

West, David, 1956-
Ghosts and other specters / illustrated by David West ; and written by Anita Ganeri.
    p. cm. — (The dark side)
Includes bibliographical references (p.   ) and index.
ISBN 978-1-61531-897-1 (library binding) — ISBN 978-1-4488-1566-1 (pbk.) — ISBN 978-1-4488-1567-8 (6-pack)
1. Ghosts—Juvenile literature. I. Ganeri, Anita, 1961- II. Title.
BF1461.W468 2011
133.1—dc22

                                                                2010003269
Printed in China

CPSIA Compliance Information: Batch #DS0102PK: For Further Information contact Rosen Publishing, New York, New York at 1-800-237-9932

Contents

Introduction

Many bizarre creatures roam the world of mythology. Their origins may be lost in the mists of history, but they have preyed on people's superstitions and imaginations since ancient times. Among them are ghosts and specters, supernatural beings from the dark side that appear in the living world. Although they cannot be touched or felt, their presence is terrifying. For thousands of years, people have claimed to have seen ghosts but what are these eerie figures? Many believe they are the souls of the dead, come back to haunt the living. Have you ever seen a ghost? Or a wraith? Or a poltergeist? Are you ready to go over to the dark side? It will send shivers down your spine . . .

Ghosts

In the spooky, gloomy twilight of a graveyard, a terrible figure emerges from the earth. It is a ghost, returning to the world of the living—the world in which you live.

The idea of ghosts is thousands of years old. This is a scene from the Old Testament of the Bible. The ghost of the prophet Samuel is shown here being summoned by the Witch of Endor.

People from cultures all over the world believe that a person's soul survives when his body dies. But sometimes the soul stays in the land of the living, perhaps because the person died in some terrible way or wants to take revenge on somebody who is still alive. In Western cultures, this soul is sometimes said to haunt a place or person and is seen as a ghost.

This is a typical medieval image of a ghost. In medieval times, when early death was more common, people were terrified by the prospect of the dead returning to them.

Ghostly Features

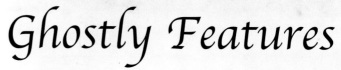

What do you think a ghost looks like? Is it a pale, transparent human figure clad in robes? Some ghosts are said to look like this, but some are invisible and some are not even human.

Any ghostly image is known as an apparition. It may be visible to one person but not another. This photograph, taken by the medium William Hope (1863–1933), is said to show a man with the ghost of his wife.

Eyewitnesses often say that ghosts appear to be made of cloudy, foglike material, so that they are see-through. That is how ghosts usually appear in photographs. Ghosts cannot be touched—you could put your hand right through a ghost. They can walk through solid objects, including walls and doors, so hiding in a room is no defense. Ghosts normally take the form of the dead person, as they were last seen, so someone who died by beheading may appear without a head or might even carry her head under her arm!

This bizarre image shows a substance apparently coming from the ear of a medium who is in contact with the spirit world. The substance is known as ectoplasm and is said to make up the ghostly body of a spirit.

Some legends tell of ghosts not of humans but of animals. The myth of the Wild Hunt (also known by various other names including the Ghost Ride, Woden's Wild Hunt, and Odin's Wild Hunt) tells of a group of ghostly hunters galloping along on ghostly horses. It is said that seeing the Wild Hunt means you are about to die or that some other terrible event is about to happen.

There are several claims of sightings of the Black Dog or Barghest, a monstrous, ghostly black hound with huge teeth and claws, which roams northern England.

Woden's Wild Hunt

Ghosts in Europe

An apparition in an English garden

Ghosts have appeared in the folklore of European countries since ancient times, when the Greeks and Romans thought that ghosts hung around burial places, doing both good and evil deeds.

The Greeks invited the ghosts of their relatives and friends to feasts. A shade was a type of ghost that featured in classical Greek stories, including Homer's *Odyssey*. Shades are spirits of the Greek underworld, which live in the shadows after death. In Roman mythology, manes (meaning "the good ones") were the souls of the dead. They were offered blood sacrifices, sometimes at gladiatorial games. The annual festival for manes was held from February 13 through 22.

A typical woman ghost, often called the White Lady (or sometimes the Gray Lady). She always appears in a long white dress.

In the Middle Ages, Europeans believed that souls went to purgatory until, as ghosts, they could make amends for their sins in life.

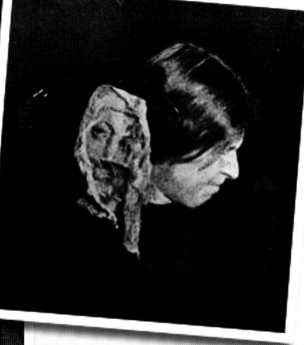

A White Lady formed from ectoplasm (see page 8)

In Britain, the White Lady is the name for a female ghost. The White Lady is often the ghost of a woman who has killed herself after losing her husband. If the White Lady appears in a family home, it means another member of the family is about to die. The Knights of Alleberg are the ghosts of twelve Swedish knights who died at the battle at Alleberg in 1389. They are said to be resting until their country needs them to fight again.

Ghosts Around the World

Ghostly figures are found in legends from all over the world, both ancient and modern. In addition, ghosts are often a feature of places of death, such as battlefields, shipwrecks, and sites of executions.

The battlefields of the American Civil War are said to be haunted by the ghosts of the fallen. In Gettysburg, Pennsylvania, where nearly 8,000 soldiers died in 1863, dozens of visitors have reported seeing ghostly wounded men and hearing the grisly sounds of battle. From Native American culture comes the *chindi*, a ghost of the Navajo people. It is said to leave a dying person's body with his last breath.

Ghosts of Civil War dead are said to haunt a rocky outcrop called Devil's Den on the battlefield at Gettysburg.

Navajo legend says that anyone who meets a chindi will fall ill with "ghost sickness."

In Japan, a funayurei *is the ghost of a person who died at sea.*

The *obambo* is a ghost of central Africa. When the obambo asks its relatives to build it a home, villagers hold a ceremony, visit the grave of the dead person, and build a small hut for the obambo. In Japan, a *yurei* is the ghost of a person who has died a violent death. It appears in white funeral robes and has black hair and lifeless hands and feet.

China has many different types of ghosts. Hungry ghosts are created when people who are greedy in life die. They gradually become weak and fade away.

Haunted Houses

Ghostly figures roam many haunted houses, castles, theaters, and other buildings around the world. These ghosts are the souls of people who have died terrible deaths in the buildings.

This house in Amityville, New York, was the scene of a terrifying haunting in the 1970s. The family who lived here fled. The haunting was the subject of a famous book and film, The Amityville Horror.

In 1974, at 112 Ocean Avenue in the town of Amityville, New York, Ronald DeFeo murdered his family as they slept. A year later the Lutz family moved into the house. But four weeks later, they moved out again, claiming that the house was haunted—perhaps by DeFeo's victims. Windows had opened and closed by themselves, doors had been ripped off their hinges, and slime had oozed through the ceilings. Mr. Lutz had even been levitated above his bed.

The ghost of President Abraham Lincoln (left) is supposed to wander the corridors of the White House (below), knocking on doors. He is also seen in the room where his old bed is kept.

The Borden house in Fall River, Massachusetts, is said to be haunted by the ghosts of two people murdered there in 1892.

The ghost of a nun was often seen walking on the grounds of the Borley Rectory. She was seen by four girls living there in 1900. The rectory burned down in 1939.

The ghosts of King Edward V and Richard, Duke of York, murdered in 1483, have been seen walking hand in hand in the Tower of London.

The Borley Rectory, in Essex, England, is known as the most haunted house in England. Reverend Smith's family lived there in the 1920s. They heard bells and footsteps, and saw lights and a ghostly horse-drawn carriage on the driveway. Ghosts are said to haunt the Tower of London. They include King Edward V and his brother the Duke of York, who were murdered there as children. Other Tower ghosts include Anne Boleyn, second wife of Henry VIII, who was beheaded in 1536.

Edward and Richard

The Brown Lady haunts the staircase of Raynham Hall, in Norfolk, England. She is the ghost of Lady Townshend.

Ghost Ships

Ghosts can be more than just humans and animals. Ghostly ships sail the oceans and ghostly trains run through the countryside. The most famous is a strange ship sailed by its ghostly captain—the Flying Dutchman.

The legend of the Flying Dutchman tells of a ship that was sunk during a storm near the Cape of Good Hope in 1641. The Flying Dutchman was its skipper, Captain Vanderdecken. As the ship went down, Vanderdecken cried out that he would pass the cape even if he had to sail until the end of time. And so he sails around the cape to this day. A sighting of the Flying Dutchman on his vessel is supposed to be a sign of impending disaster.

During World War II, the crew of a German submarine reported seeing a ghostly ship passing close by. Was it the famous Flying Dutchman?

The luxury liner RMS Queen Mary (left and below) is said to be haunted by some of the passengers who died on board.

The St. Louis Ghost Train is a strange, colored light, seen since the 1920s, that appears to move along an old rail line in Canada. Popular legend says that the light is that of a ghostly train on the line. Another ghost train, the Silverpilen ("Silver Arrow"), runs on the Stockholm subway. This legend is probably based on an unpainted silver subway train that is rarely used.

In 1879, the Tay Bridge, near Dundee, Scotland, collapsed as a train crossed, killing 75 people. Legend says that on every anniversary of the accident, a ghostly train is seen and the screams of its unfortunate passengers are heard.

Ghost Stories

Author Charles Dickens was so interested in ghosts that he joined the Ghost Club in the 1860s.

The pages of literature contain many stories of ghostly occurrences. Famous authors, including William Shakespeare, Charles Dickens, and Washington Irving, have all written ghosts into their hugely popular stories.

British Victorian author Charles Dickens used ghosts as characters in several stories, including "A Christmas Carol" (see opposite) and "The Signal-Man," a tale published in 1866 about a haunted railway worker who sees a ghost before each of three terrible accidents. "The Legend of Sleepy Hollow," by American author Washington Irving, was published in 1820. The story is set in a valley called Sleepy Hollow. Schoolteacher Ichabod Crane is haunted by a headless horseman, who is apparently the ghost of a Revolutionary War soldier.

In this 1858 painting of "The Legend of Sleepy Hollow," the Headless Horseman chases a terrified Ichabod Crane.

In William Shakespeare's *Julius Caesar*, Caesar is murdered by Brutus, who wants to control Rome. Later, Caesar's ghost appears to Brutus, saying that they will meet again on the battlefield. In Shakespeare's *Macbeth*, Macbeth kills King Duncan of Scotland. He also arranges for Banquo, a fellow general, to be killed. Banquo's ghost then appears to Macbeth at a banquet, alarming Macbeth.

The ghost of Caesar appears to Brutus in Shakespeare's play Julius Caesar.

"Yotsuya Kaidan" is a famous Japanese ghost story. In the story, the ghost of the Oiwa, a murdered woman, takes the form of a haunted lantern.

In Dickens's A Christmas Carol, *four ghosts appear to Ebenezer Scrooge on Christmas Eve. They are Jacob Marley, his dead partner, and the ghosts of Christmases Past, Present, and Future.*

Ghost Hunters

Think your house is haunted? If so, you
need to call in a team of ghost hunters
(or psychic investigators). They specialize
in detecting ghosts, recording spooky
sounds, taking photographs
and videos, and measuring all sorts
of ghostly phenomena.

A hand-held infrared temperature sensor measures the temperature of remote surfaces.

Harry Price, ghost hunter of the 1920s

Ghost hunting began at the beginning of the twentieth century, when the belief in ghosts and all things spiritual was popular. The most famous British ghost hunter of the time was Harry Price. Calling himself a paranormal researcher, he investigated the mediums, psychics, and haunted houses of the time. In 1925, he set up the National Laboratory of Psychical Research. Price became a celebrity after his work at Borley Rectory (see page 15), where some members of his team claimed to have witnessed ghostly happenings.

Modern ghost hunters carry a whole range of equipment. Basic instruments include notebooks, flashlights, sound-recording equipment, tape measures, video cameras and infrared (night vision) cameras. They also carry thermometers because ghosts are said to cool the air. A more advanced tool is an electromagnetic field (EMF) meter, used by ghost hunters to detect the electromagnetic fields that ghosts are supposed to emit. EMF meters are sometimes connected to cameras.

A ghost-hunting team investigates a haunted house. They are using their recording devices and instruments to look for evidence of ghostly activity.

A medium summons a ghost.

Ghostly Celebrations

A sinister Irish Halloween jack-o'-lantern, carved from a turnip

Traditionally, a woman can see the face of her future husband in a mirror on Halloween.

Dead souls terrify many people, but in some countries and cultures, ghosts are celebrated with special days and festivals, such as Halloween. The ghosts themselves are often invited to take part!

In ancient Britain the end of summer was celebrated on November 1. This date was also when people believed that the souls of the dead returned to Earth. They lit fires to ward off ghosts and wore disguises to keep ghosts of friends and relatives from recognizing them. This end-of-summer festival is known today as Halloween or All Hallows' Eve, when people dress up to celebrate all things spooky and ghostly. Halloween takes place on October 31 in Britain and the United States.

A Halloween celebration from the 1830s. It includes dancing and traditional games, such as bobbing for apples.

During the Chinese Ghost Festival, mourners visit graves to burn paper money, paper clothes, and other paper objects for the dead to use in the afterlife. They also eat sweets to improve their memory of the festival.

The Ghost Festival of China, or Hungry Ghost Festival, is traditionally when the ghosts of dead ancestors return to Earth to visit the living. It is always held on the fifteenth night of the seventh lunar month in the Chinese calendar. On the Day of the Dead, Mexicans (and some other peoples in South and Central America) decorate graves with candles and flowers to invite the dead to a family party. People hold street parties where they wear skull-shaped masks and eat skeleton-shaped food. The celebration is held on November 1 and 2.

A decorated skeleton called Catrina is a common sight at Day of the Dead celebrations. She is a modern version of the Lady of the Dead (an alternative name for the Mictecacihuatl, an Aztec goddess).

23

Other Specters

A giant, animated skeleton crashes through forest vegetation. It is called a *gashadokuro*, a skeleton from Japanese folklore. It is 15 times taller than a person, and if it finds you, it will bite your head off!

At a séance, a medium summons spirits from the afterlife. A specter is appearing—perhaps it is the hand of a relative of one of those people at the table.

The gashadokuro is made from the bones of people who have died of starvation. Like a ghost, such as the White Lady or the Flying Dutchman, the gashadokuro is a specter—a being from the dark side that appears and disappears in the living world. But unlike ghosts, specters do not appear in human or animal form.

This is the terrible specter of Death, known in some cultures as the Grim Reaper. He (or sometimes she) often appears as a skeleton in a hooded cape.

Poltergeists

Pots and pans, plates, and silverware flying around are a sure sign that a poltergeist is haunting a house. The word "poltergeist" comes from the German words *polten* ("making a noise") and *geist* ("ghost").

Poltergeists are invisible but noisy ghosts. Besides objects flying around, evidence of poltergeists includes rapping and crackling noises, slamming doors, moving furniture, cold spots in the air, and electric equipment failing. This scary activity is normally centered on one location, such as a haunted house. In 1948, a farmhouse in Macomb, Illinois, was burned to the ground. A poltergeist linked with the owner's niece, Wanet McNeill, who had moved to the farm against her will, was blamed.

Objects are hurled around a kitchen by an angry poltergeist.

In 1817, a poltergeist invaded the Bell household in Tennessee. The first sign of the malevolent spirit was a weird animal seen near the house. Hammering noises were followed by whispering noises that later

Betsy Bell

became shrieking. Betsy Bell's bedcovers and hair were pulled by a mysterious force.

Three New York sisters, Kate, Leah, and Margaret Fox, believed in the spirit world. In the 1840s, Kate and Margaret communicated with a poltergeist by knocking on their floorboards. As an adult, Kate could apparently move objects with spirit power.

The Fox sisters

Levitation is a form of poltergeist activity. Here, medium Colin Evans appears to levitate at a 1938 séance. He is thought to have cheated by jumping and using flash photography!

Messengers of Death

If there is one specter you don't want to see, it is a messenger of death! When a messenger of death appears, your time is up. She has come to collect your soul.

Deadly plagues and famines meant that the specter of death was ever present in the Middle Ages.

The specter of death (known as Death) features in the myths of almost all cultures. In some myths, Death actually causes death. In others, Death gathers the soul and guides it into the afterlife. Sometimes when Death appears to a person, it means he is about to die. Sometimes it means the person is already dead. In English, Death goes by the name of the Grim Reaper and appears as a cloaked skeleton (see page 25). She is also called the Angel of Death. In Scotland, a wraith is a specter connected with death.

This is La Mort du Fossoyeur *("The Death of the Grave Digger"), painted by Swiss artist Carlos Schwabe in 1895. The winged Angel of Death appears to the aged grave digger, preparing to take him into the afterlife.*

Irish and Scottish folklore features the banshee, a female spirit in the form of a hag who appears to the dying and is often seen washing the blood-stained clothes of doomed people.

Glossary

ancestors (AN-ses-terz) Family members from the past.

apparition (a-puh-RIH-shun) An appearance of a ghost or ghostlike figure.

folklore (FOHK-lawr) A collection of stories and legends attached to a particular people or place.

gladiatorial games (gla-dee-uh-TAWR-ee-ul GAYMZ) Events in Roman times at which gladiators fought each other to the death.

haunt (HONT) To visit a person or place in the form of a ghost.

legends (LEH-jendz) Traditional stories, often based on supposedly historical events.

levitated (LEH-vuh-tayt-ed) Been made to rise and float in the air, supposedly by supernatural means.

malevolent (muh-LEH-vuh-lent) Wishing or seeming to wish evil on another.

medieval (mee-DEE-vul) Relating to the Middle Ages, a period of European history from around the fifth to the fifteenth century AD.

medium (MEE-dee-um) A person who supposedly acts as a go-between between the living and the dead.

mythology (mih-THAH-luh-jee) Traditional stories, not based in historical fact but using supernatural characters to explain human behavior and natural events.

origin (OR-ih-jin) The place where things begin or from where something comes.

paranormal (pa-ruh-NOR-mul) Cannot be explained through science.

psychics (SY-kiks) People who are sensitive to forces that cannot be explained naturally.

purgatory (PUR-guh-tawr-ee) In some religious beliefs, a place of suffering or torment where souls go after death.

sacrifices (SA-kruh-fys-ez) Offerings to a god, goddess, or other being.

séance (SAY-ahnts) A meeting at which people try to receive messages from the spirits of the dead.

supernatural (soo-per-NA-chuh-rul) Having to do with magical beings, such as ghosts and fairies, and unexplained events.

transparent (tranz-PER-ent) Clear or see-through.

Further Reading

DeMolay, Jack. *Ghosts in Amityville.* New York: Rosen Publishing, 2007.

Ganeri, Anita. *An Illustrated Guide to Mythical Creatures.* New York: Hammond World Atlas, 2009.

Hamilton, Sue. *Ghosts & Goblins. World of Horror.* Edina, MN: ABDO & Daughters, 2007.

Oxlade, Chris. *The Mystery of Haunted Houses. Can Science Solve?* Chicago: Heinemann-Library, 2006.

West, David. *Ghosts and Poltergeists. Graphic Mysteries.* New York: Rosen Publishing, 2006.

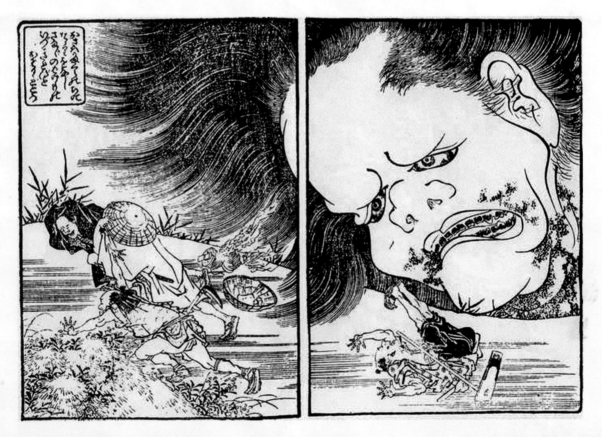

A Japanese haunting

Index

Web Sites

Due to the changing nature of Internet links, PowerKids Press has developed an online list of Web sites related to the subject of this book. This site is updated regularly. Please use this link to access the list:
www.powerkidslinks.com/darkside/ghosts/